ALLISON INDUSTRIES
A MANAGEMENT SIMULATION

Charles Stephen White
University of Tennessee—Chattanooga

IRWIN
Homewood, IL 60430
Boston, MA 02116

Printed in the United States of America.

ISBN 0-256-12906-1

1 2 3 4 5 6 7 8 9 0 ML 0 9 8 7 6 5 4 3

PREFACE

As a graduate student in business, I was required to participate in a computer-based management simulation in one of my classes. Prior to participating in the game, I believed anyone was capable of managing a business by using logic and the knowledge obtained in the pursuit of a college degree. Playing the simulation quickly changed my mind. While playing the game, I was faced with the uncertainties that all managers face in their day-to-day operations. Although I could calculate financial ratios and draw break-even graphs with absolute precision, I soon found it was not enough. I learned through the simulation that business decisions are not necessarily "right" or "wrong" but rather are "better" or "worse". After playing the simulation for one semester, I understood the intricacies of running a business better than I ever had before.

My original experience with a simulation occurred prior to the development of microcomputers. Then computers became common tools. I decided to write a computer simulation that would allow others to have the same learning experience that I had years earlier. I wanted to develop a simulation that was designed to teach the fundamentals of business. ALLISON INDUSTRIES: A MANAGEMENT SIMULATION is the result.

Allison Industries is designed to be an introductory, yet realistic simulation. In order to keep the game at an introductory level, I simulated a business that had only one product. The game still requires students to make realistic decisions, but those decisions are greatly simplified. Deciding what price to charge, how much money to borrow and how many people to hire are just a few of the real-life decisions that are characterized in the game.

In most businesses, the first day on the job is a bewildering experience. It is difficult to know what to do or how to go about doing it. Likewise, the first few rounds of the simulation will produce anxiety in most people because they haven't developed a feel for good decision making. Rest assured, the game quickly becomes comfortable to play.

The simulation is designed so that every team can be successful and make a profit if they make reasonable decisions. Learning to use the pro-forma decision sheets included in the manual will enhance the learning experience and your enjoyment of playing the game. Some of my students have told me that they enjoy the game so much they would like to continue playing after the end of the semester. I hope you feel the same way when you've finished the experience.

ACKNOWLEDGEMENTS

Thanks to the reviewers who critiqued my proposal and sample material. Their feedback and suggestions were invaluable. They are Pamela Van Epps, University of New Orleans, John Hall, University of Florida and Thomas Turk, Texas A&M University. I would also like to thank Michelle Kachur for her comments and editing. She caught many items that needed correcting and helped in the readability of the manual. Finally, I would like to thank Kurt Strand, my editor, for managing the product to publication.

DEDICATION

Thanks to my family for helping me with this project. My son, Michael, kept me laughing with endless questions about wanting to go to college so he too could play a computer game. My wife, Cindy, did the actual programming. She calmed me down many times when I thought something could not be made to work well enough to satisfy the publishers. She obviously knew her capabilities better than I did. And, finally, special thanks to little Allison who was the inspiration for this project.

ALLISON INDUSTRIES

INTRODUCTION

Allison Industries: A Management Simulation is a computer game that simulates up to three years of business activity in the microcomputer printer industry. Students usually work in teams with each team representing a different firm in the industry.

Students work together within their teams to make managerial decisions about how their firms will be run. The simulation requires teams to submit decisions in specified categories for every three-month period of the simulation (the game administrator decides how often decisions are due in real time).

Economic conditions, tax breaks and penalties simulated by *Allison Industries* and controlled by the game administrator, as well as the decisions made by your firm and the other firms in your industry, all affect the success of your firm. The object of the simulation is to plan a long-term strategy for the entire game and then use each period's decisions as tactics to help you reach your financial goals, analyzing both your mistakes and successes along the way.

HOW THE GAME IS PLAYED

All firms begin the first period of play on equal standing. At the end of each period, the simulation calculates reports for each firm, reflecting the firm's standing as a result of its decisions and industry activity. Teams use these reports to analyze the effectiveness of their previous decisions and to provide a basis for the next period's decisions. Decisions for each firm are entered into the simulation at the beginning of each period after the teams have reviewed their reports from the previous period.

The game administrator may also decide to change economic conditions or impose penalties at this point. The period is run after all firms' decisions have been collected by the game administrator. When the period has been run and three months of activity has been simulated, the simulation calculates the period's reports and the game continues.

Though future reports are provided to the team either on printout or on diskette, Period 0 reports (which are the same for all firms) are included in this manual beginning on page 8.

ALLISON INDUSTRIES: FIRM'S BACKGROUND

Allison Industries began in the early 1970's as a supplier of support items for small computers. The founder of the firm, Cruse Gillespie, began the business as a broker; that is, when someone needed parts, he knew where to find them. He sold cables, cords, small printers, and cassette recorders. It soon became apparent to Gillespie that, in the rapidly changing world of computers, personal computers were the wave of the future.

With a loan from his father-in-law, he launched *Allison Industries* (named for his daughter), making a newer and faster line of microcomputer printers. Today, *Allison Industries* manufactures and supplies only microcomputer printers.

The microcomputer industry is characterized by intense competition in a market that has historically been unable to keep up with demand. Because there are a substantial number of producers, the product tends to be price sensitive even though new printing features and capabilities are constantly being developed. The industry appears to be entering its maturity phase, with entry costs becoming prohibitive for new competitors.

Current industry analysis indicates sufficient market demand to enable all current competitors to achieve reasonable profit margins. Analysts also believe future growth in demand is possible with sufficient effort directed toward continued product development and promotion. Because the market consists of a highly technical product, current technologies have short life spans and must be continually upgraded. Therefore, the printer market has experienced continual increases in funds spent on new product development and promotion.

Production facilities have approached terminal economies of scale; that is, increasing plant capacity will not lower the unit cost of the product. Although engineering studies have indicated some areas still available for cost reductions, the number of such areas is diminishing. Product quality is a major concern in the business. For example, several firms attempted to provide maintenance agreements at a reduced price as a promotional device, but had to abandon the policy. Marketing studies indicated that customers expected defective printers to be replaced instead of repaired. In fact, some customers indicated that the presence of a maintenance agreement implied expected product failure and they subsequently changed product brand. As a result, there is little or no leeway in product quality as a strategic advantage, since all printer companies now have a policy of shipping defect-free products.

PERIOD 0 REPORTS

Shown on the following pages are the descriptions of Period 0 reports for *Allison Industries*. The Period 0 report is found on page 8. Included are the income statement, balance sheet, and ratios for period 0, as well as the average industry inputs for the same period. These reports show where *Allison Industries* stands at the beginning of the simulation.

The **income statement** provides a detailed report of your revenues and expenses over the simulated period of play.

The **balance sheet** provides an accounting of your assets and liabilities as of the end of the period of play.

The **ratio report** gives you firm's operating and financial ratios as well as the average values for the industry.

Because all firms in your industry start out in the same position as *Allison Industries,* you may refer to the reports that follow as the period 0 reports for your firm. Reports like these will be calculated for each period of the simulation.

THE INCOME STATEMENT

Every team is provided with an income statement for each period played. The Period 0 income statement is shown on Page 9. The income statement is a vital financial tool that allows a team to make future decisions affecting its ability to compete. The income statement is divided into several major sections.

REVENUES: Revenues are calculated by multiplying the number of units sold by the per-unit price. The number of units sold, however, decreases as price is increased. Revenues are converted into cash and accounts receivables.

COST OF GOODS SOLD: The firm's cost of goods sold is determined by the number of units sold multiplied by the per-unit cost of the product.

Note that cost of goods sold is not determined by the number of units produced except in the special case when production equals sales.

4

The total cost of the product is calculated by first selling as much as possible out of current production, then selling out of inventory using the LIFO (last in-first out) method. Per-unit costs are a function of the amount spent on quality control plus the firm's efficient use of capacity. The more money spent on quality control, the lower the per unit cost will be. The firm is also expected to use its plant and equipment efficiently by producing at an optimum level of approximately 80%. For example, if a firm has a capacity of 10,000 units, producing 8,000 (80%) will result in the lowest per-unit costs, all other things being equal. In no case, however, can per-unit costs drop below $200.

OPERATING EXPENSES: Operating expenses include the following factors:

1. Salaries: Salary expense equals $50,000 plus $2,500 times the number of salespeople. Since each team starts with ten salespeople, the minimum salary expense is $50,000 plus (10 X $2,500), equalling $75,000.

2. Commissions: Commission expense equals gross sales multiplied by 0.005.

3. Marketing: The team sets this amount when it inputs its decisions.

4. Research and Development: The team sets this amount when it inputs its decisions.

5. Salespeople training: This amount equals $4,000 times the number of new salespeople. It is a one-time expense.

6. Quality control: The team sets this amount when it inputs its decisions.

7.   Utilities: This amount equals the number of units of capacity times $0.40. This expense occurs whether or not the capacity is used for production.

8.   Other expense: This is an expense item the instructor uses to assess fines and penalties when teams violate the rules or procedures of the simulation. It may also be used by the instructor to provide a means for you to pay for economic information if provided.

DEPRECIATION: A plant and its equipment lose value over time. To reflect this loss of value, equipment is depreciated over time instead of being expensed against earnings immediately after being purchased.

Allison Industries charges 12% per year depreciation (3% per period). In addition, the simulation reduces the firm's actual capacity to produce by 12% per year to reflect depreciation. Thus if a firm does not replenish its capital equipment, it will find it wearing out at a rate of 3% per period. To maintain a constant production capacity, a firm would need to add 3% capacity each quarter. Depreciation is a non-cash cost; that is, depreciation will be charged against earnings to determine the amount of profit each team earns, but it will not reduce the amount of cash the firm possesses.

INTEREST EXPENSE: This is the sum of the interest charged for both regular and emergency loans. (If cash is invested in regular loan this item will appear as a negative number and will be added to the team's income instead of subtracted.)

TAXES: Taxes are calculated according to the following schedule of earnings:

EARNINGS	TAX RATE
0 - $25,000	15%
$25,001 - $50,000	18%
$50,001 - $75,000	30%
$75,001 - $100,000	40%
$100,001 and over	46%

The tax rates listed above are marginal rates; that is, the tax rate applies only to the level of income with which it is associated and not to the entire amount of income. Thus, if a team earns $200,000 in before-tax profits it will pay taxes of 15% X $25,000 plus 18% X ($50,000 minus $25,000) plus 30% X ($75,000 minus $50,000) plus 40% X ($100,000 minus $75,000) plus 46% X ($200,000 minus $100,000).

The simulation provides for a tax loss carry-forward. If a team loses money in a particular quarter, the loss incurred will be subtracted from the profits of the next quarter before the taxes are assessed. For example, if a team loses $100,000 in quarter one and earns $100,000 in quarter two, the team will pay no taxes for the two quarters since the net income for the two quarters is zero. On the following page is the Period 0 Income Statement report.

ALLISON INDUSTRIES

COMPANY
INDUSTRY
PERIOD   0

INCOME STATEMENT

REVENUES:		GROSS PROFIT	1,452,000.00
GROSS SALES	4,000,000.00	LESS:TOTAL OPER EXP	867,400.00
LESS: COGS	2,548,000.00		
		GROSS OPERATING REVENUE	584,600.00
GROSS PROFIT	1,452,000.00	LESS: DEPRECIATION	270,000.00
OPERATING EXPENSES:		EARNINGS BEFORE INTEREST	
SALARIES	75,000.00	AND TAXES	314,600.00
COMMISSIONS	20,000.00	LESS: INTEREST EXPENSE	30,600.00
MARKETING	250,000.00		
RESEARCH & DEV	500,000.00	EARNINGS BEFORE TAXES	284,000.00
SALESPERSON TRAINING	0.00	LESS: TAXES	110,390.00
QUALITY CONTROL	20,000.00		
UTILITIES	2,400.00	NET INCOME	173,610.00
TOTAL OPER EXPENSE	867,400.00		

THE BALANCE SHEET

Teams are also provided with a balance sheet for each period played. The balance sheet is divided into two major sections - (1) Assets and (2) Claims on Assets (Liabilities).

ASSETS

CASH: This reflects the amount of cash your firm has remaining at the end of the quarter. You will never have a negative cash balance because the simulation will automatically issue an emergency loan if one is needed to bring your team's cash balance to zero.

The firm earns no interest on cash. If you wish to earn interest on your cash, it must be invested in a negative regular loan. Cash may not be invested in a negative emergency loan.

ACCOUNTS RECEIVABLE: Upon selling your products your firm will receive 75% of the gross amount of the sales in cash. For example, if you sell $100,000 worth of printers in Period 3, you will receive $75,000 in cash for those sales in Period 3. The remaining 25% of your sales will be reflected in accounts receivable and will be converted to cash the next period. Therefore, using the example above, you will receive the remaining $25,000.00 of your sales in Period 4. Note, however, that in addition to receiving the $75,000.00 in Period 3 you will also receive the accounts receivables from Period 2 in cash.

The table on the next page demonstrates the cash flows resulting from sales and accounts receivables over a few periods:

9

Allison Industries

	Period 1	Period 2	Period 3	Period 4
Gross Sales	$50,000	$80,000	$100,000	$90,000
less Acct Rec	$12,500	$20,000	$ 25,000	$22,500
Cash In	$37,500	$60,000	$ 75,000	$67,500
plus prev Acct Rec	$ 0	$12,500	$ 20,000	$25,000
Total Cash	$37,500	$72,500	$ 95,000	$92,500

INVENTORIES: This amount reflects the value of unsold finished goods in inventory. Inventories occur when production has exceeded demand. The simulation does not provide for negative inventories; once a sale has been lost for lack of available product, the sale is forever lost.

The *Allison Industries* simulation uses a LIFO (last-in, first-out) inventory method. If a firm produces more than it can sell, the remaining production is placed into inventory for future sales. Although there is no "inventory carrying cost" specifically assessed for having inventories, capital costs for financing the inventories are incurred. In addition to the capital costs incurred by building up the firm's inventories, there is a substantial effect on cash flow. Inventories are not costs to be deducted from earnings, but rather are a conversion of one asset to another.

Inventories can be used as a strategic tool to prepare for anticipated future sales without adding excess capacity. Inventories can also be used to produce at optimum capacity to reduce production costs.

TOTAL CURRENT ASSETS: This amount is the sum of cash, accounts receivables, and inventories. Its value reflects the amount of short-term (or more liquid) assets.

NET PLANT AND EQUIPMENT: This value reflects the amount of capacity your firm currently possesses. If you do not add capacity, this figure will be reduced each quarter by 3% to reflect depreciation. In addition to depreciation, the value will be adjusted upward or downward depending on your sale or purchase of plant and equipment.

In order to produce a manufactured product, firms must first build the necessary plant and equipment. If a firm does not have the necessary equipment, then regardless of the level of market demand experienced, it will find itself unable to produce at a level that enables it to fill its orders. Compounding this situation is the requirement of fairly lengthy lead times to build and test production facilities. A company cannot order a factory to be built and expect the contractors to have the facilities finished quickly. The lead times involved require forecasting of future demand and capacity planning if the plant and equipment are to be operational when needed.

Allison Industries requires a one-quarter time delay between the decision to add or sell capacity and the actual implementation of the decision. Thus, if a firm decides to add capacity in Period 4, they must input the decision to add capacity in Period 3's decision set. The cash required to add capacity (or the cash received if selling) will not be deducted from your assets until the capacity is available for use. Because capacity decisions have a one-period delay, capacity decisions in the last period of the simulation are irrelevant and can have no effect on the outcome of the game.

Plant and equipment can only be built so fast, regardless of the need. *Allison Industries* allows firms to only build 5,000 units of capacity per quarter. Decisions to build more than 5,000 units are automatically reduced by the computer to the 5,000-unit limit.

11

A firm may always add capacity. Selling capacity, however, is not an option that is automatically executed. Before a firm can sell its plant and equipment, it must first find a buyer. Firms that want to sell plant and equipment indicate so in the decision set by entering a negative number for the capacity change. **The sale of capacity is only executed if other firms wish to buy plant and equipment.** If there is more capacity for sale than firms wish to buy, the sales are fairly distributed by the simulation among all firms wishing to sell. Cash-flow calculations should take into account that plant and equipment offered for sale may not in fact, be sold.

OTHER ASSETS: This is a figure that reflects assets not described above. Typical assets of this nature would be "good will" or valuable patent rights. The simulation uses this entry to correct computer rounding errors and therefore it should be a negligible amount.

TOTAL ASSETS: This amount is the sum of cash, accounts receivables, inventories, plant and equipment, and other assets. Its value reflects the total amount of the firm's assets. The absolute size of this figure does not necessarily reflect the financial health of a firm, since its value can be increased, at will, by borrowing.

CLAIMS ON ASSETS (LIABILITIES)

ACCOUNTS PAYABLE: Your firm must pay all expenses within the quarter in which they are incurred. Therefore, this figure will always equal zero.

LOANS (REGULAR AND EMERGENCY): *Allison Industries* requires cash-flow management to be accomplished through the process of borrowing and repaying funds provided by a lending institution. The simulation provides for two types of loans: regular loans and emergency loans. Regular loans can be acquired in any amount during any period and do not have to be repaid during the course of the simulation unless the game administrator directs otherwise. If you borrow money through a regular loan, you will be charged interest at the rate of **12%** per year **(3% per period)**. If a team fails to arrange their finances to leave a positive cash balance in their assets section, the computer will automatically issue an emergency loan to bring the cash balance to zero. <u>Emergency loans</u> carry an interest rate of **20%** per year **(5% per period)**. Once an emergency loan is issued, it is the team's responsibility to repay the loan. A team may choose to borrow money with a regular loan to repay the emergency loan if necessary. If a team tries to repay an emergency loan with a greater amount than the loan, the computer will automatically reduce the repayment to bring the emergency loan balance to zero.

Entering an amount in the decision set to repay the emergency loan does not guarantee that the firm will end the period with the emergency loan reduced to zero. For example, if a firm has an emergency loan, plays the period to have a negative cash flow, and fails to borrow sufficient money through a regular loan to compensate for the negative cash flow, the decision to repay the emergency loan will not result in a zero emergency loan balance. The computer will initially try to repay the old emergency loan in accordance with the decision set, but will issue a new emergency loan when it detects a negative cash balance.

Effective cash management requires that excess cash be invested in order to provide some income from the asset. Firms with positive cash balances should first attempt to repay their loans. If a firm has no debt and still finds itself with a positive cash balance, the firm can invest its excess cash in a negative regular loan. Such a loan is entered by placing a negative sign in front of the loan amount in the decision set. Negative regular loans will pay the firm interest at the rate of **12%** per year **(3% per quarter)**. The income from this type of loan is fully taxable. Firms are not allowed to carry a negative emergency loan.

TOTAL CURRENT LIABILITIES: This amount is the sum of accounts payable and all loans. It is used to reflect total debt.

RETAINED EARNINGS: Perhaps a better title for this entry on the balance sheet would be "cumulative" earnings. This figure is the sum of the firm's profit and losses over the course of the simulation. This figure reflects the firm's overall financial health better than any other information on the balance sheet. Because this simulation does not have provisions for the sale of stock with resulting distribution of profits through dividends, this entry on the balance sheet is useful for comparing firms to each other. The firm with the largest retained earnings has been the most profitable.

CONTRIBUTED CAPITAL: This entry reflects the amount of money that was invested in the firm by the owners. This amount is $8,900,000 and will not change during the simulation. The combination of retained earnings and contributed capital indicates the amount of the owner's wealth in the firm.

TOTAL CLAIMS ON ASSETS: This is the sum of total current liabilities, retained earnings, and contributed capital. This figure will be exactly equal to the "total assets" figure.

Following is an example of the firm's Period 0 balance sheet.

BALANCE SHEET

COMPANY
INDUSTRY
PERIOD 0

ASSETS		CLAIMS ON ASSETS	
CASH	863,610.00	ACCOUNTS PAYABLE	0.00
ACCOUNTS RECEIVABLE	1,000,000.00	REGULAR LOAN	1,020,000.00
INVENTORIES	0.00	EMERGENCY LOAN	0.00
TOTAL CURRENT ASSETS	1,863,610.00	TOTAL CURRENT LIABILITIES	1,020,000.00
NET PLANT & EQUIP	8,730,000.00	RETAINED EARNINGS	673,610.00
OTHER ASSETS	0.00	CONTRIBUTED CAPITAL	8,900,000.00
TOTAL ASSETS	10,593,610.00	TOTAL CLAIMS ON ASSETS	10,593,610.00

THE RATIO REPORT

The ratio report contains your firm's financial and operating ratios, averages of industry ratios, along with summary information of your firm's operations. The Period 0 Ratio Report is shown on Page 19. The following ratios are provided for each team:

Return on total assets is calculated as follows:

Return on total assets = (net income)/(total assets)

_____

Return on owner's equity is calculated as follows:

Return on owner's equity = (net income)/ (contributed capital)

_____

Return on net worth is calculated as follows:

Return on net worth = (net income)/(net worth) where:
net worth = (contributed capital) + (accumulated retained earnings)

_____

Current ratio is calculated as follows:

Current ratio = (total current assets)/(total current liabilities)

_____

Acid test ratio is calculated as follows:

> **Acid ratio = ((total current assets) - (inventories))/ (total current liabilities)**
>
> _____

Debt to total assets is calculated as follows:

> **Debt to total assets = debt/(total assets)**
>
> _____

Times interest earned is calculated as follows:

> **Times interest earned = (earnings before interest and taxes)/interest**
>
> _____

Inventory turnover is calculated as follows:

> **Inventory turnover = total revenues/inventories**
>
> _____

Total asset turnover is calculated as follows:

> **Total asset turnover = total revenues / ((total assets)+(liabilities))**
>
> _____

In addition to the ratios, the report also provides each team with the following summary information:

> Total capacity. The statement reports on your capacity prior to depreciation for the period.

Total salespeople. This is your firm's total number of salespeople as of the end of the period of play.

Sales. This is the number of units sold by your firm in the period. The dollar value of your sales is given in the income section of the report.

Inventory. Total inventory as of the end of the period is reported here. Inventory is reported in units rather than in dollars.

Cost per unit. Cost per unit for the period is reported here. Multiplying this value times the number of units produced will help you determine the cost of goods sold.

ALLISON INDUSTRIES

RATIOS: PERIOD 0

	FIRM	INDUSTRY
PROFITABILITY AND VALUATION		
Return on Total Assets	0.0164	0.0164
Return on Owners' Equity	0.0195	0.0195
Return on Net Worth	0.0181	0.0181
LIQUIDITY		
Current Ratio	1.8271	1.8271
Acid Test Ratio	1.8271	1.8271
LEVERAGE		
Debt to Total Assets	0.0963	0.0963
Times Interest Earned	10.2810	10.2810
ACTIVITY		
Inventory Turnover	0.0000	0.0000
Total Asset Turnover	0.1371	0.1371

Your firm's total capacity was 5,820 units.
Your firm's total number of salespeople is 10.
Your firm sold 7,820 units this period.
Your firm has 0 units in ending inventory.
It cost your firm $318.00 to produce one unit of inventory this period.

AVERAGE INPUTS FOR INDUSTRY   PERIOD 0

PRICE	MKTG EFF	R & D EFF	TOT SALESP	QUAL CONT
$500.00	$290,000	$620,000	10.0	$20,000

PROD'N	CAPACITY	TOT REG-L	TOT EMER-L	MKT SHARE
5,820	5,820	$1,020,000	$0	14,000

19

MAKING DECISIONS

You will work with your team members to fill out the decision sheet that lists the categories for the decisions required by the simulation. Each set of decisions is due at the time and place indicated by your instructor. If you fail to turn in your decisions for any period, the program will set the price decision to $300 and the other decisions to zero. A sample decision sheet and descriptions of each decision category follow. Decision sheets for your use are included in the appendix.

THE DECISION SHEET

The following are explanations of the decisions you will be required to make. You will make new decisions in each category at the beginning of every period. A sample of the decision sheet you will use to record your decisions is shown on page 24.

PRICE: This is the selling price of one printer. This should be a positive integer (no fractions or decimals please) greater than $300.00 and less than $2000.00. At the beginning of the game (Period 0), everyone's price is set at $500.00. The higher your price, the fewer printers you will sell.

MARKETING: This is the amount of money you want to spend over three months (you may change this amount each period) on advertising, special dealer discounts and incentives, special point-of-sale displays, and customer "factory rebates." The amount can range from $0 to any large number. It cannot be negative.

Marketing has a carry-over effect; that is, the amount of marketing effect your firm achieves is a function of this period's spending plus 20% of the amount spent in the previous period. Each team spent $250,000 on marketing in Period 0. Therefore, when deciding on the marketing amount for Period 1, keep in mind that the marketing effect will be worth the amount you enter on the decision sheet plus $50,000 (20% of period zero's $250,000 expenditure). Marketing expenditures will affect a period's sales slightly more than research and development.

RESEARCH AND DEVELOPMENT: Research and development (R&D) is money spent on developing a better product. Like marketing, the amount you spend must be a non-zero integer. Also like marketing, it has a carry-over effect. The carry-over effect for each firm is 25%. Each firm spent $500,000 on R&D in Period 0.

NEW SALESPEOPLE: These are new employees hired to sell your product. They must be trained immediately upon hiring at a cost of $4,000 each. Because you are only able to train a maximum of 15 people in any one period, you are limited to hiring no more than 15 for each period of play. Training takes effect immediately so that new salespeople begin producing sales in the same period in which they are hired. Once a salesperson has been hired, he or she is loyal and never quits. Each salesperson earns a $10,000 annual salary plus a commission of $1 on each $200 worth of sales. (1/2 of 1% based on price). Each team begins with ten salespeople on the job and no new hires.

QUALITY CONTROL: Dollars spent here increase productivity. Cost of goods sold is therefore a function of quality control. All other things being equal, the team which spends more on quality control is more likely to have a lower cost of goods sold. All teams start with a $20,000 quality control expense.

PRODUCTION: This is the number of units you wish to produce in the current period. These units are immediately available for sale. Production must be a positive number in even hundreds; if it is not in even hundreds, the program will round to the nearest hundred. Note that production cannot exceed total capacity; if it does, the program resets production to equal total capacity. Also, the cost of each unit produced depends somewhat on production. It is most efficient to run your plant near 80% of its capacity. As you deviate from this level, it costs more to produce each unit. Every team starts Period 0 with 2,000 units in inventory and producing another 5,820 units during the period (making 7,820 units total available for sale in Period 0).

CAPACITY: Capacity is the facility's maximum ability to produce. It is comprised of the plant, equipment, and anything else that allows the facility to produce units. It is expressed as the maximum number of units the production facility is able to make in one period. Capacity can be bought and sold. For instance, the facility can buy more capacity by purchasing equipment that will make more units. The maximum capacity that can be bought in any one period is 5,000 units. The decisions made each period about capacity concern only changes in capacity; you should not enter total capacity, only the amount you want to buy (a positive number evenly divisible by 100) or to sell (a negative number also evenly divisible by 100).

> *WARNING: CAPACITY CHANGES ARE EXPRESSED IN UNITS, NOT DOLLARS. ENTERING A DOLLAR AMOUNT WILL GIVE YOU 1,500 TIMES THE CAPACITY YOU WANT.*

Capacity is bought or sold at $1,500 per unit; however, you may only sell capacity if some other firm wishes to buy it. Once purchased, it becomes available for use and must be paid for in the next quarter. For example, if total capacity is 10,000 and you purchase 5,000 additional units (making 15,000 units total capacity) you may decide to produce up to 15,000 units, less 3% depreciation, in the next period after the purchase. Selling capacity also takes effect the next quarter provided that there is a buyer. Each team begins with 5,820 units of total capacity and no new purchases in Period 0.

REGULAR LOAN: A regular loan is money borrowed from the bank. The maximum loan you may take out in any period is $15,000,000. You may borrow money by entering a positive whole number as your regular loan decision. Interest rates are 12% per annum on this type of loan. The amount on your decision sheet is the amount you want to **add** to your total loan, **not the total loan**. If you wish to pay back all or part of your loan, enter a negative number. Each team begins with a $1,000,000 regular loan already outstanding and borrows another $20,000 in Period 0, making $1,020,000 total borrowed. If you have excess cash, you may invest it by taking out a "negative loan"; that is, you may carry a negative amount in loans so the bank (the computer) pays you 12%.

EMERGENCY LOAN: This loan is automatically granted by the program when you run out of cash. Interest on this type of loan is 20% per annum. You are responsible for paying it back, with a negative entry in the "Emergency Loan" decision. (Be careful not to enter a positive number; if you do, you will be <u>borrowing</u> money at 20%). There is no credit limit on emergency loans.

VERIFICATION TOTAL: This is a number used to be sure you (if you are using diskette input) or the game administrator (if you hand in decisions on paper) have correctly entered all the inputs. This number is calculated by adding up the numbers in all of your decisions for each period. It has no meaning other than detecting errors. If the program's verification total and yours do not agree, a data entry error may have occurred. If this happens, you may reenter your decisions without penalty. Be careful to add negative numbers correctly: 12 + (-3) = 9, not 15!!

Following is a copy of the decision sheet with sample entries and the verification total accurately completed. Subsequent copies can be found in the Appendix.

23

DECISION SHEET
ALLISON INDUSTRIES

Firm __3__

Industry __B__

Period __6__

Price (>+ $300)

| | | | | | | 7 | 0 | 0 |

Marketing (>= $0)

| | | | 1 | 6 | 0 | 0 | 0 |

R AND D (>=$ 0)

| | | | 9 | 5 | 0 | 0 | 0 |

New Salespersons (0 – 15)

| 0 | 3 |

Quality Control (>= $0)

| | | | 4 | 5 | 0 | 0 | 0 |

Production Units
(>= 0, in even hundreds,
enter 200 as 200, not 2)

| | | | | 7 | 4 | 0 | 0 |

Capacity Changes
(use negative if selling,
positive if buying.
Must be in even 100's)

| | | | | 1 | 4 | 0 | 0 |

Regular Loan
(positive if borrowing,
negative for repayment)

| | | 1 | 7 | 2 | 0 | 0 | 0 |

Emergency Loan

| | – | 1 | 2 | 2 | 6 | 8 | 1 |

Verification Total
(Add up all of the above
numbers: watch negatives:
7 + (–2) = 5, not 9)

| | | 3 | 5 | 8 | 8 | 2 | 2 |

PLANNING FOR DECISION MAKING

Your decisions each period should be part of an overall strategy for your firm. Implementing an overall strategy requires you to base your decisions upon sound estimates of future operations. The following sections contain forms designed to assist you in the preparation of forecasts and estimates of cash, production levels, inventory, and profits. Specifically included are sections on:

1. Production planning. This section will assist you in forecasting your firm's requirements for plant capacity. Capacity decisions can affect your ability to implement strategies requiring high levels of production.

2. Cash-flow analysis. Cash flow analysis will help you determine the amount of money you need to borrow in order to prevent your firm from incurring an emergency loan. Teams with excess cash can invest their funds in a negative loan which will increase their profits.

3. Pro forma statements. Pro forma forms are provided so that you can prepare forecasted financial and operating statements. These statements help determine if your firm's strategy is achieving the team's goals.

4. Break-even analysis. This section can help you decide if your production strategy is feasible. Graphical representation of the break-even equations provide a visual picture of your firm's profit potential.

25

PRODUCTION PLANNING

Production efficiency is determined largely by the amount of time spent on planning. By taking into account both historical data and future needs, you can determine the necessary quantities of product to be produced during the next business period.

On page 28 is a worksheet designed to help you plan and implement production strategies. Filling out a similar worksheet each period will provide information on your firm's ability to accurately forecast product demand, which is valuable when making operating and marketing decisions. Additional worksheets appear in the appendix. Use the top half of the worksheet to calculate your firm's total available capacity for the current period. Following are directions on how to correctly complete the production planning worksheet.

1. Begin by entering on the first line the capacity given to you on the last period's Ratio Report. Express all numbers on the worksheet in terms of numbers of units rather than dollar values.

2. The simulation reduces each team's capacity by 3% each period to represent the physical depreciation machines undergo. Therefore you will need to subtract 3% from capacity to get the current period's beginning capacity.

3. Capacity added in the last period takes effect at the beginning of this period. If your firm added capacity in the last period, add the number of units purchased to the capacity calculated in step 2. If your firm sold capacity in the last period, subtract. This gives you the total capacity you have to work with in this period. Use the lower half of the worksheet to determine how many units will be available for sale and to project how many units will be sold in the current period.

4.   You may produce as many units as you have capacity to produce.   If you try to overproduce, the simulation will automatically adjust your decision so you can only produce up to your capacity. To achieve the lowest per-unit cost you should produce 80% of capacity.

5.   In addition to the units produced each quarter, you may also sell from your inventory.   Inventory figures are provided on the summary information below the ratio report.   Add previous inventory to current production to determine the team's total units available for sale.

6.   Subtracting anticipated sales from total goods available for sale will give an estimate of the team's ending inventory for the quarter. After the period is run, you can compare the estimated ending inventory to the actual results obtained after the period is run. This will determine if the forecasting models you are using to project sales are accurate.   By keeping track of your projections along with the actual sales results, you will have a strong base of data upon which to build and improve your strategy for production and capacity planning.

After the period is run, you can compare the estimated ending inventory to the actual results obtained after the period is run, This will determine if the forecasting models you are using to project sales are accurate. By keeping track of your projections along with the actual sales results, you will have a strong base of data upon which to build and improve your strategy for production and capacity planning. Following is a copy of the production planning worksheet. Copies for use can be found in the Appendix.

PRODUCTION PLANNING WORKSHEET

PERIOD_____

Last period's beginning capacity	_____ units
Less: 3% depreciation	_____ units
Beginning Capacity (this period)	_____ units
Plus: Added capacity from last period	_____ units
TOTAL AVAILABLE CAPACITY	_____ units
Production (must be equal to or less than available capacity)	_____ units
Plus: Inventory from last period	_____ units
TOTAL UNITS AVAILABLE FOR SALE =	_____ units
Less: Anticipated sales	_____ units
Ending Inventory	_____ units

CASH-FLOW ANALYSIS

Cash is the life blood of a business. The absence of cash can bring a thriving operation to a standstill. When vendors, workers, and utilities are not paid when due, they retract their services with little notice. Businesses operating at substantial losses (negative profit) can remain in business through the power of positive cash flow alone; that is, as long as the firm has cash it can remain in business. Therefore, a fundamental function of management is to ensure that the firm has sufficient cash to operate.

Cash management can be viewed from either a short-term or a long-term perspective. From the most short-term perspective, cash is necessary to pay current liabilities. As the financial perspective moves from the short term toward the longer term, the firm may hold assets in less liquid forms (see Figure 1). Examples of liquid assets in industry include inventories and short-term securities of other firms. Less-liquid assets would include fixed plant and equipment, which would be depreciated over their useful life. A primary objective of financial management is to balance the liquidity of assets with the requirements for the firm's liabilities. If adequate liquidity is maintained, short-term debt and expenses can be paid. Less-liquid assets can be held for longer-term debt.

LIQUIDITY GRAPH

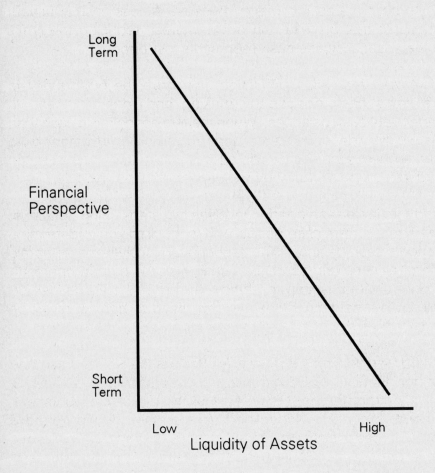

One strategy that ensures a firm the ability to meet short-term debt is to maintain excess cash balances. This strategy does not prove to be in a company's best interests, however, because excess cash is usually held in accounts that provide little or no interest, reducing the firm's return on the asset. Excess cash represents lost opportunity.

Within the *Allison Industries* simulation, you have the opportunity to manage a firm's cash position by making and repaying loans to maintain adequate cash balances. When the firm needs more cash than operations will provide, such as for plant expansion or inventory build up, you can request a loan. If excess cash is anticipated, the funds can be invested in a "negative loan" by repayment of loans not owed.

Determining the firm's cash position involves two steps. First, you must analyze the firm's current cash position. This requires you to determine the last period's cash balance. The second step involves the algebraic summation of all uses and sources of cash over the current operating period. To help with this step, cash-flow worksheets are provided so you can determine how much cash you will need to borrow or will be able to repay on your loans.

Exhibits 1 and 2 show Firm 1's reports for Periods 2 & 3. The cash flow worksheet for Firm 1 would be filled out as shown in Exhibit 3. Beginning cash from Period 2 is entered at the top of the worksheet. To this amount, income is added and uses of cash during Period 3 subtracted. Sources of cash include net income, depreciation, accounts receivable (from the previous period), net inventory change, and increases in loans. Uses of cash include current period's accounts receivable, new plant, and repayment of loans. The worksheets supplied allows you to enter the sources and uses of cash into a format that simplifies the calculations. Copies of the cash flow worksheet for your use are in the Appendix.

31

Exhibit 1

ALLISON INDUSTRIES

COMPANY 1
INDUSTRY C
PERIOD 2
INCOME STATEMENT

REVENUES:		GROSS PROFIT	3,691,456.94
GROSS SALES	5,744,700.00	LESS:TOTAL OPER EXP	657,077.92
LESS: COGS	2,053,243.06		
		GROSS OPERATING REVENUE	3,034,379.02
GROSS PROFIT	3,691,456.94	LESS: DEPRECIATION	389,043.00
OPERATING EXPENSES:		EARNINGS BEFORE INTEREST	
SALARIES	75,000.00	AND TAXES	2,645,336.02
COMMISSIONS	28,723.50	LESS: INTEREST EXPENSE	30,600.00
MARKETING	200,000.00		
RESEARCH & DEV	300,000.00	EARNINGS BEFORE TAXES	2,614,736.02
SALESPERSON TRAINING	0.00	LESS: TAXES	1,182,528.59
QUALITY CONTROL	50,000.00		
UTILITIES	3,354.42	NET INCOME	1,432,207.43
TOTAL OPER EXPENSE	657,077.92		

BALANCE SHEET

COMPANY 1
INDUSTRY C
PERIOD 2

ASSETS		CLAIMS ON ASSETS	
CASH	0.00	ACCOUNTS PAYABLE	0.00
ACCOUNTS RECEIVABLE	1,436,175.00	REGULAR LOAN	1,020,000.00
INVENTORIES	198,472.65	EMERGENCY LOAN	331,260.77
TOTAL CURRENT ASSETS	1,634,647.65	TOTAL CURRENT LIABILITIES	1,351,260.77
NET PLANT & EQUIP	12,579,057.86	RETAINED EARNINGS	3,962,443.88
OTHER ASSETS	(0.86)	CONTRIBUTED CAPITAL	8,900,000.00
TOTAL ASSETS	14,213,704.65	TOTAL CLAIMS ON ASSETS	14,213,704.65

Exhibit 2

ALLISON INDUSTRIES

COMPANY 1
INDUSTRY C
PERIOD 3
INCOME STATEMENT

REVENUES:		GROSS PROFIT	4,420,591.11
GROSS SALES	6,855,300.00	LESS:TOTAL OPER EXP	662,530.28
LESS: COGS	2,434,708.89		
		GROSS OPERATING REVENUE	3,758,060.83
GROSS PROFIT	4,420,591.11	LESS: DEPRECIATION	377,371.73
OPERATING EXPENSES:		EARNINGS BEFORE INTEREST	
SALARIES	75,000.00	AND TAXES	3,380,689.10
COMMISSIONS	34,276.50	LESS: INTEREST EXPENSE	30,650.43
MARKETING	200,000.00		
RESEARCH & DEV	300,000.00	EARNINGS BEFORE TAXES	3,350,038.67
SALESPERSON TRAINING	0.00	LESS: TAXES	1,520,767.82
QUALITY CONTROL	50,000.00		
UTILITIES	3,253.78	NET INCOME	1,829,270.85
TOTAL OPER EXPENSE	662,530.28		

BALANCE SHEET

COMPANY 1
INDUSTRY C
PERIOD 3

ASSETS		CLAIMS ON ASSETS	
CASH	1,797,465.24	ACCOUNTS PAYABLE	0.00
ACCOUNTS RECEIVABLE	1,713,825.00	REGULAR LOAN	1,020,000.00
INVENTORIES	0.00	EMERGENCY LOAN	1,260.77
TOTAL CURRENT ASSETS	3,511,290.24	TOTAL CURRENT LIABILITIES	1,021,260.77
NET PLANT & EQUIP	12,201,686.48	RETAINED EARNINGS	5,791,714.74
OTHER ASSETS	(1.21)	CONTRIBUTED CAPITAL	8,900,000.00
TOTAL ASSETS	15,712,975.51	TOTAL CLAIMS ON ASSETS	15,712,975.51

Exhibit 3

CASH FLOW WORKSHEET

PERIOD _____3_____

BEGINNING CASH _____0_____
(Cash on last period's
balance sheet)

CHANGES
RESULTING
FROM
OPERATIONS

Plus NET INCOME 1,829,271

Plus DEPRECIATION 377,372

Less ACCOUNTS RECEIVABLE 1,713,825

Plus ACCOUNTS RECEIVABLE 1,436,175
(from last period)

INVENTORY CHANGES

CHANGES

last period's inv 198,473
Less - this period's inv 0

IN

Plus NET INVENTORY CHANGE 198,473

ASSETS

Less NEW PLANT 0
(Plant ordered
last period, enter
negative if sold)

CHANGES

Plus NEW LOANS 0
(enter negative

IN
if repaying)

LIABILITIES Less EMERGENCY LOAN REPAID 330,000

CASH THIS PERIOD 1,797,466

PRO FORMA STATEMENTS

A pro forma income statement is an educated guess of what will occur; it is created before the firm's actual operations are conducted. A pro forma income statement shows how the actual statement will look if certain assumptions are realized. As a management tool, a pro forma statement allows managers to look into the future and see the results of different price and production strategies before they are implemented. Managers can better anticipate profits from operations, cash flows, and changes in financial structure, while the possibility of engaging in strategies with foreseeable problems is reduced. For example, if a pro forma statement indicates the firm will suffer substantial losses based on certain decisions, a new set of decisions can be tried.

A pro forma worksheet can be set up on a microcomputer based spreadsheet that allows the analyst to do "what if" analyses. "What if" analyses are done by trying many different strategies of price and expense combinations. Though "what if" analyses can be done manually, the microcomputer can complete the calculations quickly, so many different ideas can be tested. Ideas that have the most merit can then be used in a set of actual decisions. Pro forma cash-flow statements can be used to determine the amount of loans needed for the next period, which can keep cash balances at a minimum.

Pro forma statements are based on both assumptions and on known facts. For example, when forecasting the firm's revenues, one needs to know both the per-unit price and the number of units sold. The per-unit price is known with absolute precision, since the price is set by you. In question is the number of units to be sold during the pro forma period. In some cases this information is also known with precision. For example, companies that consistently sell all of their production each period can estimate the number of units to be sold with little guesswork. Only firms engaging in new strategies or faced with inconsistent decisions by their competitors need to worry about the absolute accuracy of their assumptions concerning the number of units to be sold.

Just as revenues can be forecast with precision, so can expenses. Most expenses in the simulation are input decisions, such as the firm's marketing expense or research and development costs. Knowing the amount of expenses incurred plus knowing the revenues expected allows the decision maker to accurately calculate future profits, taxes, and inventories.

Pro forma worksheets like the sample shown on page 35, follow the general format of the income statement used in *Allison Industries* and are included in the Appendix. You can use the income statement worksheet as a model for a pro forma balance sheet.

Once you have used the pro forma income statement and balance sheet to determine which decisions have the most merit, you can use the information provided as direct input into the cash flow worksheets provided earlier. Comparison of the results of decisions with the pro forma statements will enable you to develop better strategies throughout the term of the simulation. Following is a pro forma income statement. Copies for use can be found in the Appendix.

PRO FORMA INCOME STATEMENT

PERIOD _____

REVENUES:
  GROSS SALES (price/unit * # units sold)   _____
    LESS: COGS (cost/unit * # units sold)   _____

GROSS PROFIT   _____

OPOERATING EXPENSES:
   SALARIES   _____
   COMMISSIONS (gross sales * 0.005)   _____
   MARKETING   _____
   RESEARCH & DEVELOPMENT   _____
   SALESPERSON TRAINING (new salesp. * $4000)   _____
   QUALITY CONTROL   _____
   UTILITIES (0.40 * units of capacity)   _____
   OTHER EXPENSE   _____
TOTAL OPERATING EXPENSES   _____

GROSS PROFIT   _____
   LESS: TOTAL OPERATING EXPENSES   _____

GROSS OPERATING REVENUE   _____
   LESS: DEPRECIATION   _____

EARNINGS BEFORE INTEREST AND TAXES   _____
   LESS: INTEREST EXPENSE   _____

EARNINGS BEFORE TAXES   _____
   LESS: TAXES (see tax table)   _____

NET INCOME   _____

BREAKEVEN ANALYSIS

One of the fundamental questions you, as a manager, should ask is whether a prospective business has the potential of surviving and providing the rewards appropriate for the risk incurred. The answer to this question depends upon the company's ability to earn a profit. To answer this question, you must calculate the company's breakeven sale's quantity and compare this figure with estimated sales. If future sales are estimated to be greater than the break even quantity, you are justified in beginning the venture. If estimated sales are less than breakeven, you must find other ways of conducting the business if it is to be profitable.

The primary analysis of break even involves the determination of a sales quantity that will yield neither a profit nor a loss; that is, a quantity that will just "break even" (See Figure 2).

BREAKEVEN ANALYSIS

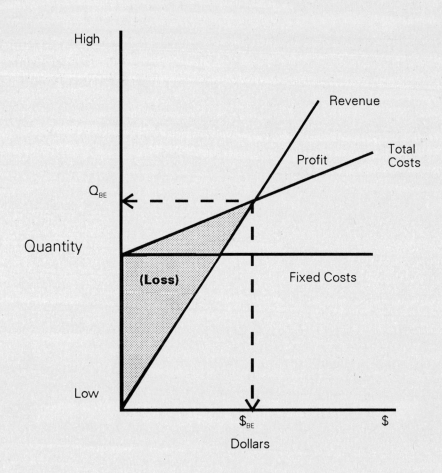

To determine this quantity we start with a definition of profit.

PROFIT = REVENUES - EXPENSES

Determining revenues for a single-product firm requires a knowledge of the number of units to be sold and of the price per unit. Therefore:

REVENUES = Sales quantity X Price per unit

Calculating a firm's expenses requires two calculations, since companies incur two types of expenses. The first type of expense is called "fixed costs" and includes expenses that are independent of sales quantity. These are costs that remain the same whether the firm sells zero units or sells everything it can make. Examples of fixed costs are executive salaries, rent payments, and liability insurance. *Allison Industries* has fixed costs made up of marketing expenses, research and development expense, training costs, quality control expenses, depreciation, and interest.

FIXED COSTS = Operating expenses + Depreciation + Interest

The second type of expense is called a "variable cost," and includes costs that are dependent on sales quantity. Direct labor and material used in production are examples of variable costs. The simulation expresses this amount in the "cost per unit" value provided in the summary information section of the ratio report. Therefore:

VARIABLE COSTS = Sales quantity X Cost per unit

Variable costs are not incurred until the product is actually sold. Therefore, producing a product and placing it into inventory does not constitute a cost until it is sold.

The equations for breakeven can be calculated as follows:

$$PROFIT = REVENUES - EXPENSES$$

therefore:

$$PROFIT = (\text{Sales quantity} \times \text{Price per unit}) - EXPENSES$$

$$PROFIT = (\text{Sales quantity} \times \text{Price per unit}) - (\text{Fixed costs} + \text{Variable costs})$$

$$PROFIT = (\text{Sales quantity} \times \text{Price per unit}) - (\text{Fixed costs} + (\text{Sales quantity} \times \text{cost per unit}))$$

To find the breakeven quantity, profit is set to zero.

$$0 = (\text{Sales quantity} \times \text{Price per unit}) - (\text{Fixed costs} + (\text{Sales quantity} \times \text{cost per unit}))$$

The objective of these calculations is to find the sales quantity necessary to produce zero profit. Solving the equation for sales quantity yields:

$$\text{SALES QUANTITY} = \text{Fixed costs}/(\text{sales price} - \text{cost per unit})$$

Looking at Period 0's financial reports, we calculate the breakeven quantity as followings:

Price = \$500.00
Variable cost per unit = \$318.00
Fixed costs = Total operating expenses + Depreciation + Interest

41

Allison Industries

Therefore:
Fixed costs = $866,878 + $270,000 + $30,600
Fixed costs = $1,167,478

Breakeven sales quantity = $1,167,478/($500/unit - $318/unit)

Breakeven sales quantity = 6,415 units

Given a price of $500 and expenses listed above, sales of less than 6,415 units will produce a loss. As mentioned earlier, breakeven analysis has primary value in determining whether or not to go into a new business. Since the simulation assumes you are already in business and will continue throughout the semester, the analysis is more useful to you in determining appropriate capacity, pricing, and operating strategies. Trying different values of price, capacity, and expenses in breakeven analysis will allow you to better select a strategy that yields profitable operations.

INPUT AND OUTPUT

ENTERING YOUR DECISIONS

Your instructor has chosen the way in which you will turn in your decisions -- either on diskette if the class has access to personal computers, or on paper. Please read the appropriate section below for the method chosen.

ON PAPER: Make your decisions and write them on one of the decision sheets provided in the appendix. Be sure to fill in your industry, team, and period. Clearly indicate negative numbers with a minus sign. Make your entries legible and be sure your verification total is correct. Keep a copy for yourself, since your instructor may keep your original.

42

ON DISKETTE: It will help if you write your team's decisions on one of the decision sheets included in the appendix to make it easier to enter the information into the computer. Team members should take turns entering the data onto the diskette so everyone learns the procedure.

To enter your decisions into the computer and onto your diskette you will need the following things:

1. An IBM PC (or compatible) computer (a printer is not necessary).

2. A DOS (Disk Operating System) diskette.

3. Your team's simulation diskette.

4. A blank diskette to use as your backup.

5. A copy of your decisions.

STEP 1

Hard Drive computers: After booting the microcomputer, place your diskette in Drive A and type A: and press the return key. The screen prompt will appear like this: A>_ (the underscore will flash).

Floppy Drive computers: Put the DOS diskette into disk drive A and shut the drive door. Turn the computer on. Turn on your monitor (TV screen). (NOTE: some monitors do not have an on/off control, but automatically come on when the computer starts to work). After you have turned the computer on, you may get messages asking you to enter the date and time, or you may get a prompt like this: A>_ (the underscore will flash). If you are asked for date and time, enter them. The date is entered in as MM-DD-YY where MM is the month (01-12),

DD is the day (01-31) and YY is the last two digits of the year. Time is entered as HH:MM:SS (notice the colons instead of dashes) where HH is the hour (00-23), MM is for minutes (00-59), and SS is for seconds (0-59).

STEP 2

Once you get the A> prompt the computer is asking you for information. Put your team's diskette into Drive A and close the door. (Note: If your computer will not accept your type of diskette in Drive A, place the diskette into Drive B instead. Type B: and press the return key.) Now type **DECIDE** and press the return key. You are up and running.

STEP 3

Follow the instructions on the computer's screen. After you enter your decisions, the program will automatically list the decisions recorded for all periods of play. If you need to change a decision after you've entered it on the diskette, rerun the program and enter ALL the decisions over again, using the same period number. The program will erase the old (incorrect) decisions.

STEP 4

Once you have entered your decisions, you should make a backup copy of your diskette. To do this, place your diskette in Drive A and the backup diskette into Drive B. Type the following:

COPY A:*.* B:

and press the return key. Note that there is a space between the word "copy" and the "A:" above and that there are no spaces in the A:*.* part of the command.

GETTING YOUR REPORTS

Reports are calculated for each firm at the end of every period. Like decisions, they may be communicated either on paper or on diskette.

ON PAPER: If you hand in your decisions on paper, you will get your output on paper. Your instructor will give you further details about when and where to receive your results.

ON DISKETTE: If you have handed in your decisions on diskette, you may receive your output on your diskette, too. To get a copy of your output, you will need:

1.   A microcomputer with a printer.

2.   Your diskette with the output on it.

Place your diskette in a disk drive. Turn on the printer and check to see that it is "on line." Type one of the following commands:

> If your disk is in Drive A:, type:
> **COPY A:reportX.Y LPT1:** (return)

> If your disk is in Drive B:, type:
> **COPY B:reportX.Y LPT1:** (return)

The name of your file depends on (X) your firm number and (Y) the period number. The format for the file name is:

"REPORT" + "firmnumber" + "." + "period number"

For example, if you are firm 2 and this is Period 5 then your file name is REPORT2.5 (no spaces).

THE MOST COMMON QUESTIONS STUDENTS ASK

QUESTION #1:   Can we change our decisions?

ANSWER: You may change your input decisions as often as you like prior to turning them in to the game administrator by rerunning the program on the student diskette. However, once the decisions have been turned in to the game administrator you may not change them.

QUESTION #2:   Can I use my computer at home to play the game?

ANSWER: Yes. You can also use a home computer to get copies of your output by typing the following command:

COPY REPORTX.Y LPT1: (return)

where X is your team number and Y is the period number of the report you wish to copy to the printer.

QUESTION #3:   Are there any "tricks" to the game?

ANSWER: No. The simulation is merely a set of equations designed to represent business conditions. There is no "right" or "wrong" way to make decisions, although there are better and worse ways to compete.

QUESTION #4:   Do I need to know how to program computers?

ANSWER: No. The simulation requires no programming of any type. If your instructor uses diskette input, it is helpful to know the fundamentals of operating a microcomputer so that you can get your financial reports more easily.

47

QUESTION #5:   <u>What happens if I turn in my decisions late?</u>

ANSWER: Late decisions cannot be accepted by the simulation. If decisions are not turned in on time, the simulation will enter a price of $300 and set every other decision to zero.

FOR DISKETTE USERS ONLY

QUESTION #6:   <u>Why do I need to turn in two diskettes?</u>

ANSWER: Occasionally, diskettes fail. By providing two diskettes you guard yourself against this potential problem. If your primary diskette fails, a backup copy allows the professor to input your decisions. Without the backup copy in hand, the professor must either rerun the simulation at a later time or set your decisions to default values.

QUESTION #7:   <u>Why do I need to turn in a decision sheet if I already have my decisions on diskette?</u>

ANSWER: On rare occasions diskettes will fail in a manner that allows them to be used even though they contain faulty information. By providing a paper document, you are demonstrating to the professor that your decision set was previously determined with an accurate verification total. The decision sheet can also be attached to the paper copy of your financial reports for future analysis.

Appendix

DECISION SHEET
ALLISON INDUSTRIES

Firm _____

Industry _____

Period _____

Price (>+ $300)

Marketing (>= $0)

R AND D (>=$ 0)

New Salespersons (0 – 15)

Quality Control (>= $0)

Production Units
(>= 0, in even hundreds,
enter 200 as 200, not 2)

Capacity Changes
(use negative if selling,
positive if buying.
Must be in even 100's)

Regular Loan
(positive if borrowing,
negative for repayment)

Emergency Loan

Verification Total
(Add up all of the above
numbers: watch negatives:
7 + (-2) = 5, not 9)

DECISION SHEET
ALLISON INDUSTRIES

Firm _____
Industry _____
Period _____

Price (>+ $300)

Marketing (>= $0)

R AND D (>=$ 0)

New Salespersons (0 – 15)

Quality Control (>= $0)

Production Units
(>= 0, in even hundreds,
enter 200 as 200, not 2)

Capacity Changes
(use negative if selling,
positive if buying.
Must be in even 100's)

Regular Loan
(positive if borrowing,
negative for repayment)

Emergency Loan

Verification Total
(Add up all of the above
numbers: watch negatives:
7 + (–2) = 5, not 9)

DECISION SHEET
ALLISON INDUSTRIES

Firm _____
Industry _____
Period _____

Price (>+ $300)

Marketing (>= $0)

R AND D (>=$ 0)

New Salespersons (0 – 15)

Quality Control (>= $0)

Production Units
(>= 0, in even hundreds,
enter 200 as 200, not 2)

Capacity Changes
(use negative if selling,
positive if buying.
Must be in even 100's)

Regular Loan
(positive if borrowing,
negative for repayment)

Emergency Loan

Verification Total
(Add up all of the above
numbers: watch negatives:
7 + (−2) = 5, not 9)

DECISION SHEET
ALLISON INDUSTRIES

Firm _____

Industry _____

Period _____

Price (>+ $300)

Marketing (>= $0)

R AND D (>=$ 0)

New Salespersons (0 – 15)

Quality Control (>= $0)

Production Units
(>= 0, in even hundreds,
enter 200 as 200, not 2)

Capacity Changes
(use negative if selling,
positive if buying.
Must be in even 100's)

Regular Loan
(positive if borrowing,
negative for repayment)

Emergency Loan

Verification Total
(Add up all of the above
numbers: watch negatives:
7 + (−2) = 5, not 9)

DECISION SHEET
ALLISON INDUSTRIES

Firm _____
Industry _____
Period _____

Price (>+ $300)

Marketing (>= $0)

R AND D (>=$ 0)

New Salespersons (0 – 15)

Quality Control (>= $0)

Production Units
(>= 0, in even hundreds,
enter 200 as 200, not 2)

Capacity Changes
(use negative if selling,
positive if buying.
Must be in even 100's)

Regular Loan
(positive if borrowing,
negative for repayment)

Emergency Loan

Verification Total
(Add up all of the above
numbers: watch negatives:
7 + (-2) = 5, not 9)

DECISION SHEET
ALLISON INDUSTRIES

Firm _____

Industry _____

Period _____

Price (>+ $300)

Marketing (>= $0)

R AND D (>=$ 0)

New Salespersons (0 – 15)

Quality Control (>= $0)

Production Units
(>= 0, in even hundreds,
enter 200 as 200, not 2)

Capacity Changes
(use negative if selling,
positive if buying.
Must be in even 100's)

Regular Loan
(positive if borrowing,
negative for repayment)

Emergency Loan

Verification Total
(Add up all of the above
numbers: watch negatives:
7 + (–2) = 5, not 9)

DECISION SHEET
ALLISON INDUSTRIES

Firm _____

Industry _____

Period _____

Price (>+ $300)

Marketing (>= $0)

R AND D (>=$ 0)

New Salespersons (0 – 15)

Quality Control (>= $0)

Production Units
(>= 0, in even hundreds,
enter 200 as 200, not 2)

Capacity Changes
(use negative if selling,
positive if buying.
Must be in even 100's)

Regular Loan
(positive if borrowing,
negative for repayment)

Emergency Loan

Verification Total
(Add up all of the above
numbers: watch negatives:
7 + (−2) = 5, not 9)

DECISION SHEET
ALLISON INDUSTRIES

Firm _____

Industry _____

Period _____

Price (>+ $300)

Marketing (>= $0)

R AND D (>=$ 0)

New Salespersons (0 – 15)

Quality Control (>= $0)

Production Units
(>= 0, in even hundreds,
enter 200 as 200, not 2)

Capacity Changes
(use negative if selling,
positive if buying.
Must be in even 100's)

Regular Loan
(positive if borrowing,
negative for repayment)

Emergency Loan

Verification Total
(Add up all of the above
numbers: watch negatives:
7 + (-2) = 5, not 9)

DECISION SHEET
ALLISON INDUSTRIES

Firm _____

Industry _____

Period _____

Price (>+ $300)

Marketing (>= $0)

R AND D (>=$ 0)

New Salespersons (0 – 15)

Quality Control (>= $0)

Production Units
(>= 0, in even hundreds,
enter 200 as 200, not 2)

Capacity Changes
(use negative if selling,
positive if buying.
Must be in even 100's)

Regular Loan
(positive if borrowing,
negative for repayment)

Emergency Loan

Verification Total
(Add up all of the above
numbers: watch negatives:
7 + (-2) = 5, not 9)

DECISION SHEET
ALLISON INDUSTRIES

Firm _____

Industry _____

Period _____

Price (>+ $300)

Marketing (>= $0)

R AND D (>=$ 0)

New Salespersons (0 – 15)

Quality Control (>= $0)

Production Units
(>= 0, in even hundreds,
enter 200 as 200, not 2)

Capacity Changes
(use negative if selling,
positive if buying.
Must be in even 100's)

Regular Loan
(positive if borrowing,
negative for repayment)

Emergency Loan

Verification Total
(Add up all of the above
numbers: watch negatives:
7 + (−2) = 5, not 9)

DECISION SHEET
ALLISON INDUSTRIES

Firm _____

Industry _____

Period _____

Price (>+ $300)

Marketing (>= $0)

R AND D (>=$ 0)

New Salespersons (0 – 15)

Quality Control (>= $0)

Production Units
(>= 0, in even hundreds,
enter 200 as 200, not 2)

Capacity Changes
(use negative if selling,
positive if buying.
Must be in even 100's)

Regular Loan
(positive if borrowing,
negative for repayment)

Emergency Loan

Verification Total
(Add up all of the above
numbers: watch negatives:
7 + (-2) = 5, not 9)

DECISION SHEET
ALLISON INDUSTRIES

Firm _____

Industry _____

Period _____

Price (>+ $300)

Marketing (>= $0)

R AND D (>=$ 0)

New Salespersons (0 – 15)

Quality Control (>= $0)

Production Units
(>= 0, in even hundreds,
enter 200 as 200, not 2)

Capacity Changes
(use negative if selling,
positive if buying.
Must be in even 100's)

Regular Loan
(positive if borrowing,
negative for repayment)

Emergency Loan

Verification Total
(Add up all of the above
numbers: watch negatives:
7 + (−2) = 5, not 9)

PRO FORMA INCOME STATEMENT

PERIOD _____

REVENUES: _____
  GROSS SALES (price/unit * # units sold)   _____
   LESS: COGS (cost/unit * # units sold)

GROSS PROFIT   _____

OPOERATING EXPENSES:
  SALARIES
  COMMISSIONS (gross sales * 0.005)   _____
  MARKETING   _____
  RESEARCH & DEVELOPMENT   _____
  SALESPERSON TRAINING (new salesp. * $4000)   _____
  QUALITY CONTROL   _____
  UTILITIES (0.40 * units of capacity)   _____
  OTHER EXPENSE   _____
TOTAL OPERATING EXPENSES   _____

GROSS PROFIT   _____
  LESS: TOTAL OPERATING EXPENSES   _____

GROSS OPERATING REVENUE   _____
  LESS: DEPRECIATION   _____

EARNINGS BEFORE INTEREST AND TAXES   _____
  LESS: INTEREST EXPENSE   _____

EARNINGS BEFORE TAXES   _____
  LESS: TAXES (see tax table)   _____

NET INCOME   _____

PRO FORMA INCOME STATEMENT

PERIOD _____

REVENUES:
  GROSS SALES (price/unit * # units sold)   _____
    LESS: COGS (cost/unit * # units sold)   _____

GROSS PROFIT   _____

OPOERATING EXPENSES:
    SALARIES
    COMMISSIONS (gross sales * 0.005)   _____
    MARKETING   _____
    RESEARCH & DEVELOPMENT   _____
    SALESPERSON TRAINING (new salesp. * $4000)   _____
    QUALITY CONTROL   _____
    UTILITIES (0.40 * units of capacity)   _____
    OTHER EXPENSE   _____
TOTAL OPERATING EXPENSES   _____

GROSS PROFIT   _____
    LESS: TOTAL OPERATING EXPENSES   _____

GROSS OPERATING REVENUE   _____
    LESS: DEPRECIATION   _____

EARNINGS BEFORE INTEREST AND TAXES   _____
    LESS: INTEREST EXPENSE   _____

EARNINGS BEFORE TAXES   _____
    LESS: TAXES (see tax table)   _____

NET INCOME   _____

PRO FORMA INCOME STATEMENT

PERIOD _____

REVENUES:
  GROSS SALES (price/unit * # units sold)   _____
    LESS: COGS (cost/unit * # units sold)

GROSS PROFIT   _____

OPOERATING EXPENSES:
    SALARIES
    COMMISSIONS (gross sales * 0.005)   _____
    MARKETING   _____
    RESEARCH & DEVELOPMENT   _____
    SALESPERSON TRAINING (new salesp. * $4000) _____
    QUALITY CONTROL   _____
    UTILITIES (0.40 * units of capacity)   _____
    OTHER EXPENSE   _____
TOTAL OPERATING EXPENSES   _____

GROSS PROFIT   _____
    LESS: TOTAL OPERATING EXPENSES   _____

GROSS OPERATING REVENUE   _____
    LESS: DEPRECIATION   _____

EARNINGS BEFORE INTEREST AND TAXES   _____
    LESS: INTEREST EXPENSE   _____

EARNINGS BEFORE TAXES   _____
    LESS: TAXES (see tax table)   _____

NET INCOME   _____

PRO FORMA INCOME STATEMENT

PERIOD _____

REVENUES:
  GROSS SALES (price/unit * # units sold)   _____
    LESS: COGS (cost/unit * # units sold) _____

GROSS PROFIT   _____

OPOERATING EXPENSES:
  SALARIES
  COMMISSIONS (gross sales * 0.005)   _____
  MARKETING   _____
  RESEARCH & DEVELOPMENT   _____
  SALESPERSON TRAINING (new salesp. * $4000) _____
  QUALITY CONTROL   _____
  UTILITIES (0.40 * units of capacity)   _____
  OTHER EXPENSE   _____
TOTAL OPERATING EXPENSES   _____

GROSS PROFIT
  LESS: TOTAL OPERATING EXPENSES   _____

GROSS OPERATING REVENUE
  LESS: DEPRECIATION   _____

EARNINGS BEFORE INTEREST AND TAXES
  LESS: INTEREST EXPENSE   _____

EARNINGS BEFORE TAXES
  LESS: TAXES (see tax table)   _____

NET INCOME   _____

PRO FORMA INCOME STATEMENT

PERIOD _____

REVENUES:
  GROSS SALES (price/unit * # units sold)   _____
    LESS: COGS (cost/unit * # units sold)   _____

GROSS PROFIT   _____

OPOERATING EXPENSES:
   SALARIES
   COMMISSIONS (gross sales * 0.005)   _____
   MARKETING   _____
   RESEARCH & DEVELOPMENT   _____
   SALESPERSON TRAINING (new salesp. * $4000)   _____
   QUALITY CONTROL   _____
   UTILITIES (0.40 * units of capacity)   _____
   OTHER EXPENSE   _____
TOTAL OPERATING EXPENSES   _____

GROSS PROFIT
   LESS: TOTAL OPERATING EXPENSES   _____

GROSS OPERATING REVENUE
   LESS: DEPRECIATION   _____

EARNINGS BEFORE INTEREST AND TAXES
   LESS: INTEREST EXPENSE   _____

EARNINGS BEFORE TAXES
   LESS: TAXES (see tax table)   _____

NET INCOME   _____

PRO FORMA INCOME STATEMENT

PERIOD _____

REVENUES:
  GROSS SALES (price/unit * # units sold)   _____
    LESS: COGS (cost/unit * # units sold)   _____

GROSS PROFIT   _____

OPOERATING EXPENSES:
    SALARIES
    COMMISSIONS (gross sales * 0.005)   _____
    MARKETING   _____
    RESEARCH & DEVELOPMENT   _____
    SALESPERSON TRAINING (new salesp. * $4000) _____
    QUALITY CONTROL   _____
    UTILITIES (0.40 * units of capacity)   _____
    OTHER EXPENSE   _____
TOTAL OPERATING EXPENSES   _____

GROSS PROFIT
    LESS: TOTAL OPERATING EXPENSES   _____
                                   _____

GROSS OPERATING REVENUE
    LESS: DEPRECIATION   _____
                                   _____

EARNINGS BEFORE INTEREST AND TAXES
    LESS: INTEREST EXPENSE   _____
                                   _____

EARNINGS BEFORE TAXES
    LESS: TAXES (see tax table)   _____
                                   _____

NET INCOME   ==================

PRO FORMA INCOME STATEMENT

PERIOD _____

REVENUES:
  GROSS SALES (price/unit * # units sold) _____
   LESS: COGS (cost/unit * # units sold) _____

GROSS PROFIT _____

OPOERATING EXPENSES:
   SALARIES
   COMMISSIONS (gross sales * 0.005) _____
   MARKETING _____
   RESEARCH & DEVELOPMENT _____
   SALESPERSON TRAINING (new salesp. * $4000) _____
   QUALITY CONTROL _____
   UTILITIES (0.40 * units of capacity) _____
   OTHER EXPENSE _____
TOTAL OPERATING EXPENSES _____

GROSS PROFIT
   LESS: TOTAL OPERATING EXPENSES _____
_____

GROSS OPERATING REVENUE _____
   LESS: DEPRECIATION _____

EARNINGS BEFORE INTEREST AND TAXES _____
   LESS: INTEREST EXPENSE _____

EARNINGS BEFORE TAXES _____
   LESS: TAXES (see tax table) _____

NET INCOME ================

PRO FORMA INCOME STATEMENT

PERIOD _____

REVENUES:
  GROSS SALES (price/unit * # units sold)   _____
    LESS: COGS (cost/unit * # units sold)   _____

GROSS PROFIT   _____

OPOERATING EXPENSES:
    SALARIES
    COMMISSIONS (gross sales * 0.005)   _____
    MARKETING   _____
    RESEARCH & DEVELOPMENT   _____
    SALESPERSON TRAINING (new salesp. * $4000) _____
    QUALITY CONTROL   _____
    UTILITIES (0.40 * units of capacity)   _____
    OTHER EXPENSE   _____
TOTAL OPERATING EXPENSES   _____

GROSS PROFIT   _____
    LESS: TOTAL OPERATING EXPENSES   _____

GROSS OPERATING REVENUE   _____
    LESS: DEPRECIATION   _____

EARNINGS BEFORE INTEREST AND TAXES   _____
    LESS: INTEREST EXPENSE   _____

EARNINGS BEFORE TAXES   _____
    LESS: TAXES (see tax table)   _____

NET INCOME   _____

PRO FORMA INCOME STATEMENT

PERIOD _____

REVENUES:
  GROSS SALES (price/unit * # units sold)   _____
   LESS: COGS (cost/unit * # units sold)   _____

GROSS PROFIT   _____

OPOERATING EXPENSES:
  SALARIES
  COMMISSIONS (gross sales * 0.005)   _____
  MARKETING   _____
  RESEARCH & DEVELOPMENT   _____
  SALESPERSON TRAINING (new salesp. * $4000) _____
  QUALITY CONTROL   _____
  UTILITIES (0.40 * units of capacity)   _____
  OTHER EXPENSE   _____
TOTAL OPERATING EXPENSES   _____

GROSS PROFIT
  LESS: TOTAL OPERATING EXPENSES   _____

GROSS OPERATING REVENUE
  LESS: DEPRECIATION   _____

EARNINGS BEFORE INTEREST AND TAXES
  LESS: INTEREST EXPENSE   _____

EARNINGS BEFORE TAXES
  LESS: TAXES (see tax table)   _____

NET INCOME   =================

PRO FORMA INCOME STATEMENT

PERIOD _____

REVENUES:
  GROSS SALES (price/unit * # units sold)   _____
    LESS: COGS (cost/unit * # units sold)   _____

GROSS PROFIT   _____

OPOERATING EXPENSES:
   SALARIES
   COMMISSIONS (gross sales * 0.005)   _____
   MARKETING   _____
   RESEARCH & DEVELOPMENT   _____
   SALESPERSON TRAINING (new salesp. * $4000)   _____
   QUALITY CONTROL   _____
   UTILITIES (0.40 * units of capacity)   _____
   OTHER EXPENSE   _____
TOTAL OPERATING EXPENSES   _____

GROSS PROFIT
   LESS: TOTAL OPERATING EXPENSES   _____

GROSS OPERATING REVENUE
   LESS: DEPRECIATION   _____

EARNINGS BEFORE INTEREST AND TAXES
   LESS: INTEREST EXPENSE   _____

EARNINGS BEFORE TAXES
   LESS: TAXES (see tax table)   _____

NET INCOME   =====================

PRO FORMA INCOME STATEMENT

PERIOD _____

REVENUES:
  GROSS SALES (price/unit * # units sold)   _____
    LESS: COGS (cost/unit * # units sold)

GROSS PROFIT   _____

OPOERATING EXPENSES:
    SALARIES
    COMMISSIONS (gross sales * 0.005)   _____
    MARKETING   _____
    RESEARCH & DEVELOPMENT   _____
    SALESPERSON TRAINING (new salesp. * $4000) _____
    QUALITY CONTROL   _____
    UTILITIES (0.40 * units of capacity)   _____
    OTHER EXPENSE   _____
TOTAL OPERATING EXPENSES   _____

GROSS PROFIT   _____
    LESS: TOTAL OPERATING EXPENSES   _____

GROSS OPERATING REVENUE   _____
    LESS: DEPRECIATION   _____

EARNINGS BEFORE INTEREST AND TAXES   _____
    LESS: INTEREST EXPENSE   _____

EARNINGS BEFORE TAXES   _____
    LESS: TAXES (see tax table)   _____

NET INCOME   _____

PRO FORMA INCOME STATEMENT

PERIOD _____

REVENUES:
  GROSS SALES (price/unit * # units sold)   _____
    LESS: COGS (cost/unit * # units sold)   _____

GROSS PROFIT   _____

OPOERATING EXPENSES:
  SALARIES
  COMMISSIONS (gross sales * 0.005)   _____
  MARKETING   _____
  RESEARCH & DEVELOPMENT   _____
  SALESPERSON TRAINING (new salesp. * $4000)   _____
  QUALITY CONTROL   _____
  UTILITIES (0.40 * units of capacity)   _____
  OTHER EXPENSE   _____
TOTAL OPERATING EXPENSES   _____

GROSS PROFIT
  LESS: TOTAL OPERATING EXPENSES   _____

GROSS OPERATING REVENUE
  LESS: DEPRECIATION   _____

EARNINGS BEFORE INTEREST AND TAXES
  LESS: INTEREST EXPENSE   _____

EARNINGS BEFORE TAXES
  LESS: TAXES (see tax table)   _____

NET INCOME   _____

CASH FLOW WORKSHEET

PERIOD _____

BEGINNING CASH   _____
(Cash on last period's
balance sheet)

CHANGES   Plus   NET INCOME   _____
RESULTING
FROM   Plus   DEPRECIATION   _____
OPERATIONS
    Less   ACCOUNTS RECEIVABLE   _____

    Plus   ACCOUNTS RECEIVABLE   _____
(from last period)

INVENTORY CHANGES

CHANGES
       last period's inv _____
IN   Less - this period's inv _____

    Plus   NET INVENTORY CHANGE _____
ASSETS
    Less   NEW PLANT   _____
(Plant ordered
last period, enter
negative if sold)

CHANGES   Plus   NEW LOANS   _____
(enter negative
IN   if repaying)

LIABILITIES   Less   EMERGENCY LOAN REPAID _____

CASH THIS PERIOD   _____

CASH FLOW WORKSHEET

PERIOD _____

BEGINNING CASH _____
(Cash on last period's
balance sheet)

CHANGES RESULTING FROM OPERATIONS			
	Plus	NET INCOME	_____
	Plus	DEPRECIATION	_____
	Less	ACCOUNTS RECEIVABLE	_____
	Plus	ACCOUNTS RECEIVABLE (from last period)	_____

INVENTORY CHANGES

CHANGES

IN

ASSETS

last period's inv _____
Less - this period's inv _____

Plus   NET INVENTORY CHANGE   _____

Less   NEW PLANT   _____
(Plant ordered
last period, enter
negative if sold)

CHANGES

IN

LIABILITIES

Plus   NEW LOANS   _____
(enter negative
if repaying)

Less   EMERGENCY LOAN REPAID _____

CASH THIS PERIOD   _____

CASH FLOW WORKSHEET

PERIOD   _____

                           BEGINNING CASH   _____
                           (Cash on last period's
                           balance sheet)

CHANGES   Plus   NET INCOME   _____
RESULTING
FROM   Plus   DEPRECIATION   _____
OPERATIONS
               Less   ACCOUNTS RECEIVABLE   _____

               Plus   ACCOUNTS RECEIVABLE   _____
                        (from last period)

INVENTORY CHANGES

CHANGES   last period's inv   _____
               Less - this period's inv   _____
IN

               Plus   NET INVENTORY CHANGE   _____
ASSETS
               Less   NEW PLANT   _____
                        (Plant ordered
                        last period, enter
                        negative if sold)

CHANGES   Plus   NEW LOANS   _____
                        (enter negative
IN   if repaying)

LIABILITIES   Less   EMERGENCY LOAN REPAID   _____

                           CASH THIS PERIOD   _____

CASH FLOW WORKSHEET

PERIOD _____

		BEGINNING CASH (Cash on last period's balance sheet)	_____
CHANGES RESULTING FROM OPERATIONS	Plus	NET INCOME	_____
	Plus	DEPRECIATION	_____
	Less	ACCOUNTS RECEIVABLE	_____
	Plus	ACCOUNTS RECEIVABLE (from last period)	_____

INVENTORY CHANGES

CHANGES IN ASSETS		last period's inv Less - this period's inv	_____
	Plus	NET INVENTORY CHANGE	_____
	Less	NEW PLANT (Plant ordered last period, enter negative if sold)	_____
CHANGES IN LIABILITIES	Plus	NEW LOANS (enter negative if repaying)	_____
	Less	EMERGENCY LOAN REPAID	_____
		CASH THIS PERIOD	_____

CASH FLOW WORKSHEET

PERIOD _____

BEGINNING CASH   _____
(Cash on last period's
balance sheet)

CHANGES RESULTING FROM OPERATIONS			
	Plus	NET INCOME	_____
	Plus	DEPRECIATION	_____
	Less	ACCOUNTS RECEIVABLE	_____
	Plus	ACCOUNTS RECEIVABLE (from last period)	_____

INVENTORY CHANGES

CHANGES IN ASSETS			
		last period's inv _____	
	Less –	this period's inv _____	
	Plus	NET INVENTORY CHANGE	_____
	Less	NEW PLANT (Plant ordered last period, enter negative if sold)	_____

CHANGES IN LIABILITIES			
	Plus	NEW LOANS (enter negative if repaying)	_____
	Less	EMERGENCY LOAN REPAID	_____

CASH THIS PERIOD   _____

CASH FLOW WORKSHEET

PERIOD   _____

BEGINNING CASH   _____
(Cash on last period's
balance sheet)

CHANGES   Plus   NET INCOME   _____
RESULTING
FROM   Plus   DEPRECIATION   _____
OPERATIONS
   Less   ACCOUNTS RECEIVABLE   _____

   Plus   ACCOUNTS RECEIVABLE   _____
(from last period)

INVENTORY CHANGES

CHANGES   last period's inv _____
   Less - this period's inv _____
IN

   Plus   NET INVENTORY CHANGE   _____
ASSETS
   Less   NEW PLANT   _____
(Plant ordered
last period, enter
negative if sold)

CHANGES   Plus   NEW LOANS   _____
(enter negative
IN   if repaying)

LIABILITIES   Less   EMERGENCY LOAN REPAID   _____

CASH THIS PERIOD   _____

CASH FLOW WORKSHEET

PERIOD _____

BEGINNING CASH   _____
(Cash on last period's
balance sheet)

CHANGES   Plus   NET INCOME   _____
RESULTING
FROM   Plus   DEPRECIATION   _____
OPERATIONS
                 Less   ACCOUNTS RECEIVABLE   _____

                 Plus   ACCOUNTS RECEIVABLE   _____
                        (from last period)

INVENTORY CHANGES

CHANGES   last period's inv _____
                 Less - this period's inv _____
IN
                 Plus   NET INVENTORY CHANGE   _____
ASSETS
                 Less   NEW PLANT   _____
                        (Plant ordered
                        last period, enter
                        negative if sold)

CHANGES   Plus   NEW LOANS   _____
                        (enter negative
IN   if repaying)

LIABILITIES   Less   EMERGENCY LOAN REPAID   _____

                        CASH THIS PERIOD   _____

CASH FLOW WORKSHEET

PERIOD _____

BEGINNING CASH _____
(Cash on last period's
balance sheet)

CHANGES
RESULTING
FROM
OPERATIONS

Plus NET INCOME _____

Plus DEPRECIATION _____

Less ACCOUNTS RECEIVABLE _____

Plus ACCOUNTS RECEIVABLE _____
(from last period)

INVENTORY CHANGES

CHANGES

IN

ASSETS

       last period's inv _____
Less – this period's inv _____

Plus NET INVENTORY CHANGE _____

Less NEW PLANT _____
(Plant ordered
last period, enter
negative if sold)

CHANGES

IN

LIABILITIES

Plus NEW LOANS _____
(enter negative
if repaying)

Less EMERGENCY LOAN REPAID _____

CASH THIS PERIOD _____

CASH FLOW WORKSHEET

PERIOD _____

		BEGINNING CASH (Cash on last period's balance sheet)	_____
CHANGES RESULTING FROM OPERATIONS	Plus	NET INCOME	_____
	Plus	DEPRECIATION	_____
	Less	ACCOUNTS RECEIVABLE	_____
	Plus	ACCOUNTS RECEIVABLE (from last period)	_____

INVENTORY CHANGES

CHANGES IN ASSETS		last period's inv _____	
	Less -	this period's inv _____	
	Plus	NET INVENTORY CHANGE	_____
	Less	NEW PLANT (Plant ordered last period, enter negative if sold)	_____
CHANGES IN LIABILITIES	Plus	NEW LOANS (enter negative if repaying)	_____
	Less	EMERGENCY LOAN REPAID	_____
		CASH THIS PERIOD	_____

CASH FLOW WORKSHEET

PERIOD _____

BEGINNING CASH _____
(Cash on last period's
balance sheet)

CHANGES   Plus   NET INCOME _____
RESULTING
FROM   Plus   DEPRECIATION _____
OPERATIONS
   Less   ACCOUNTS RECEIVABLE _____

   Plus   ACCOUNTS RECEIVABLE _____
           (from last period)

INVENTORY CHANGES

CHANGES   last period's inv _____
   Less - this period's inv _____
IN

   Plus   NET INVENTORY CHANGE _____
ASSETS
   Less   NEW PLANT _____
           (Plant ordered
           last period, enter
           negative if sold)

CHANGES   Plus   NEW LOANS _____
           (enter negative
IN   if repaying)

LIABILITIES   Less   EMERGENCY LOAN REPAID _____

CASH THIS PERIOD _____

CASH FLOW WORKSHEET

PERIOD   _____

BEGINNING CASH   _____
(Cash on last period's
balance sheet)

CHANGES   Plus   NET INCOME   _____
RESULTING
FROM   Plus   DEPRECIATION   _____
OPERATIONS
    Less   ACCOUNTS RECEIVABLE   _____

    Plus   ACCOUNTS RECEIVABLE   _____
           (from last period)

INVENTORY CHANGES

CHANGES   last period's inv _____
    Less – this period's inv _____
IN

    Plus   NET INVENTORY CHANGE   _____
ASSETS
    Less   NEW PLANT   _____
           (Plant ordered
           last period, enter
           negative if sold)

CHANGES   Plus   NEW LOANS   _____
           (enter negative
IN   if repaying)

LIABILITIES   Less   EMERGENCY LOAN REPAID   _____

CASH THIS PERIOD   _____

CASH FLOW WORKSHEET

PERIOD _____

                          BEGINNING CASH _____
                          (Cash on last period's
                          balance sheet)

CHANGES RESULTING FROM OPERATIONS	<u>Plus</u>	NET INCOME	_____
	<u>Plus</u>	DEPRECIATION	_____
	<u>Less</u>	ACCOUNTS RECEIVABLE	_____
	<u>Plus</u>	ACCOUNTS RECEIVABLE (from last period)	_____

INVENTORY CHANGES

CHANGES		<u>last period's inv</u>	
IN	Less -	this period's inv	
	<u>Plus</u>	NET INVENTORY CHANGE	_____
ASSETS	<u>Less</u>	NEW PLANT (Plant ordered last period, enter negative if sold)	_____

CHANGES IN LIABILITIES	<u>Plus</u>	NEW LOANS (enter negative if repaying)	_____
	<u>Less</u>	EMERGENCY LOAN REPAID	_____

                          CASH THIS PERIOD _____

PRODUCTION PLANNING WORKSHEET

PERIOD _____

Last period's beginning capacity   _____ units

    Less: 3% depreciation   _____ units

Beginning Capacity (this period)   _____ units

    Plus: Added capacity from last period   _____ units

TOTAL AVAILABLE CAPACITY   _____ units

Production (must be equal to or less than   _____ units
    available capacity)

    Plus: Inventory from last period   _____ units

TOTAL UNITS AVAILABLE FOR SALE =   _____ units

    Less: Anticipated sales   _____ units

Ending Inventory   _____ units

PRODUCTION PLANNING WORKSHEET

PERIOD _____

Last period's beginning capacity   _____ units

    Less: 3% depreciation   _____ units

Beginning Capacity (this period)   _____ units

    Plus: Added capacity from last period   _____ units

TOTAL AVAILABLE CAPACITY   _____ units

Production (must be equal to or less than   _____ units
    available capacity)

    Plus: Inventory from last period   _____ units

TOTAL UNITS AVAILABLE FOR SALE =   _____ units

    Less: Anticipated sales   _____ units

Ending Inventory   _____ units

PRODUCTION PLANNING WORKSHEET

PERIOD _____

Last period's beginning capacity   _____ units

    Less: 3% depreciation   _____ units

Beginning Capacity (this period)   _____ units

    Plus: Added capacity from last period   _____ units

TOTAL AVAILABLE CAPACITY   _____ units

Production (must be equal to or less than   _____ units
       available capacity)

    Plus: Inventory from last period   _____ units

TOTAL UNITS AVAILABLE FOR SALE =   _____ units

    Less: Anticipated sales   _____ units

Ending Inventory   _____ units

PRODUCTION PLANNING WORKSHEET

PERIOD _____

Last period's beginning capacity   _____ units

    Less: 3% depreciation   _____ units

Beginning Capacity (this period)   _____ units

    Plus: Added capacity from last period   _____ units

TOTAL AVAILABLE CAPACITY   _____ units

Production (must be equal to or less than   _____ units
    available capacity)

    Plus: Inventory from last period   _____ units

TOTAL UNITS AVAILABLE FOR SALE =   _____ units

    Less: Anticipated sales   _____ units

Ending Inventory   _____ units

PRODUCTION PLANNING WORKSHEET

PERIOD _____

Last period's beginning capacity   _____ units

    Less: 3% depreciation   _____ units

Beginning Capacity (this period)   _____ units

    Plus: Added capacity from last period   _____ units

TOTAL AVAILABLE CAPACITY   _____ units

Production (must be equal to or less than   _____ units
      available capacity)

    Plus: Inventory from last period   _____ units

TOTAL UNITS AVAILABLE FOR SALE =   _____ units

    Less: Anticipated sales   _____ units

Ending Inventory   _____ units

PRODUCTION PLANNING WORKSHEET

PERIOD_____

Last period's beginning capacity   _____ unit

    Less: 3% depreciation   _____ unit

Beginning Capacity (this period)   _____ units

    Plus: Added capacity from last period   _____ units

TOTAL AVAILABLE CAPACITY   _____ units

Production (must be equal to or less than   _____ units
    available capacity)

    Plus: Inventory from last period   _____ units

TOTAL UNITS AVAILABLE FOR SALE =   _____ units

    Less: Anticipated sales   _____ units

Ending Inventory   _____ units

PRODUCTION PLANNING WORKSHEET

PERIOD _____

Last period's beginning capacity	_____	units
Less: 3% depreciation	_____	units
Beginning Capacity (this period)	_____	units
Plus: Added capacity from last period	_____	units
TOTAL AVAILABLE CAPACITY	_____	units
Production must be equal to or less than available capacity)	_____	units
Plus: Inventory from last period	_____	units
TOTAL UNITS AVAILABLE FOR	_____	units
Less: Anticipated sales	_____	units
Ending Inventory	_____	units

PRODUCTION PLANNING WORKSHEET

PERIOD_____

Last period's beginning capacity   _____ units

    Less: 3% depreciation   _____ units

Beginning Capacity (this period)   _____ units

    Plus: Added capacity from last period   _____ units

TOTAL AVAILABLE CAPACITY   _____ units

Production (must be equal to or less than   _____ units
       available capacity)

    Plus: Inventory from last period   _____ units

TOTAL UNITS AVAILABLE FOR SALE =   _____ units

    Less: Anticipated sales   _____ units

Ending Inventory   _____ units

PRODUCTION PLANNING WORKSHEET

PERIOD _____

Last period's beginning capacity   _____ units

     Less: 3% depreciation   _____ units

Beginning Capacity (this period)   _____ units

     Plus: Added capacity in last period   _____ units

TOTAL AVAILABLE CAPACITY   _____ units

Production (must be equal to or less than   _____ u.
     available capacity)

     Plus: Inventory from last period   _____ units

TOTAL UNITS AVAILABLE FOR SALE =   _____ units

     Less: Anticipated sales   _____ units

Ending Inventory   _____ units

PRODUCTION PLANNING WORKSHEET

PERIOD _____

Last period's beginning capacity   _____ units

   Less: 3% depreciation   _____ units

Beginning Capacity (this period)   _____ units

   Plus: Added capacity from last period   _____ units

TOTAL AVAILABLE CAPACITY   _____ units

Production (must be equal to or less than   _____ u__
         available capacity)

   Plus: Inventory from last period   _____ units

TOTAL UNITS AVAILABLE FOR SALE =   _____ units

   Less: Anticipated sales   _____ units

Ending Inventory   _____ units

PRODUCTION PLANNING WORKSHEET

PERIOD_____

Last period's beginning capacity   _____ units

   Less: 3% depreciation   _____ units

Beginning Capacity (this period)   _____ units

   Plus: Added capacity from last period _____ units

TOTAL AVAILABLE CAPACITY   _____ units

Production (must be equal to or less than _____ units
   available capacity)

   Plus: Inventory from last period   _____ units

TOTAL UNITS AVAILABLE FOR SALE =   _____ units

   Less: Anticipated sales   _____ units

Ending Inventory   _____ units

PRODUCTION PLANNING WORKSHEET

PERIOD _____

Last period's beginning capacity   _____ units

    Less: 3% depreciation   _____ units

Beginning Capacity (this period)   _____ nits

    Plus: Added capacity from last period   _____ u⏐ s

TOTAL AVAILABLE CAPACITY   _____ units

Production (must be equal to or less than   _____ units
available capacity)

    Plus: Inventory from last period   _____ units

TOTAL UNITS AVAILABLE FOR SALE =   _____ units

    Less: Anticipated sales   _____ units

Ending Inventory   _____ units